A **SMITHSONIAN** COLORING BOOK

# NATIVE AMERICANS

Illustrations and Text by Peter F. Copeland

Smithsonian Institution Press
Washington, D.C.

Consultant for this book:
Herman J. Viola, Director, National Anthropological Archives, Department of Anthropology, National Museum of Natural History. Advice and support were provided by Kathy S. Borrus and Norma Ryan of the Smithsonian Museum Shops.

# INTRODUCTION

From Tierra del Fuego at the southernmost tip of South America to the Arctic regions of North America, a wide and colorful variety of Native American peoples and cultures flourished at the time of their discovery by Europeans. The Hall of Eskimo and Indian Cultures in the National Museum of Natural History is filled with exhibits of many of these Native Americans—organized according to cultural areas. The drawings in this coloring book are based on current and—in some cases—former displays in that hall.

Many of the Indian and Eskimo objects in the Smithsonian collections were acquired during the nineteenth century by explorers, missionaries, members of the armed forces, Indian agents, and professional anthropologists.

Featured in this book are Woodland, Plains, Northwest Coast, California, and southwestern United States Indians; peoples from the West Indies, Guatemala, the Andes, and Patagonia; and also representatives of the polar Eskimos.

**Eskimo Seal Hunters** The Eskimos in the Arctic look to the sea for most of their subsistence. From the large aquatic animals they obtain food, skins for clothing, blubber for lamps, and bone and ivory for tools and weapons.

**Eskimo Clothing** The northernmost people of the world, the polar Eskimos wear a variety of warm clothing. The woman's costume here is of squirrel skins; the man wears a suit of caribou skins.

**Caribou-hunting Indians** In the northern pine forests live nomadic tribes whose main resource is the caribou. They also hunt and trap deer, beaver, and hare, and they fish in the lakes and streams. Although true Indians, they have many costumes that resemble those of their Arctic neighbors, the Eskimos.

**Seminole Indians of the Everglades** These Indians, an offshoot of the Creek Nation of Georgia, withdrew to the swamplands of south Florida after the Seminole War in the first half of the 19th century. They lived in small villages, remote from white settlements, by hunting, fishing, gathering wild plants, and raising corn.

**Plains Indians Hunting Buffalo** This method of hunting was used by the Indians of the Great Plains before they had horses, which were brought to America by the Spaniards. A young man, disguised as a buffalo, lured a herd over the edge of a cliff. Other hunters kept the buffalo moving by flapping buffalo skins at them. At the base of the cliff, still other hunters killed the buffalo with spears and arrows.

**Captain John Smith and the Powhatan Indians** The famous English adventurer and colonist trades with Powhatan Indians on the James River in Virginia in 1607. These Indians traded food and skins with Captain John Smith and his fellow explorers in exchange for colored beads, cloth, and mirrors.

**Plains Indian Dress, 1890** The man on the right is from the Blackfoot tribe. He is wearing a horned bonnet, shirt, and leggings decorated with weasel skin pendants. The Sioux woman in the center wears a buckskin dress and a leather belt ornamented with beadwork. At left is a Sioux warrior.

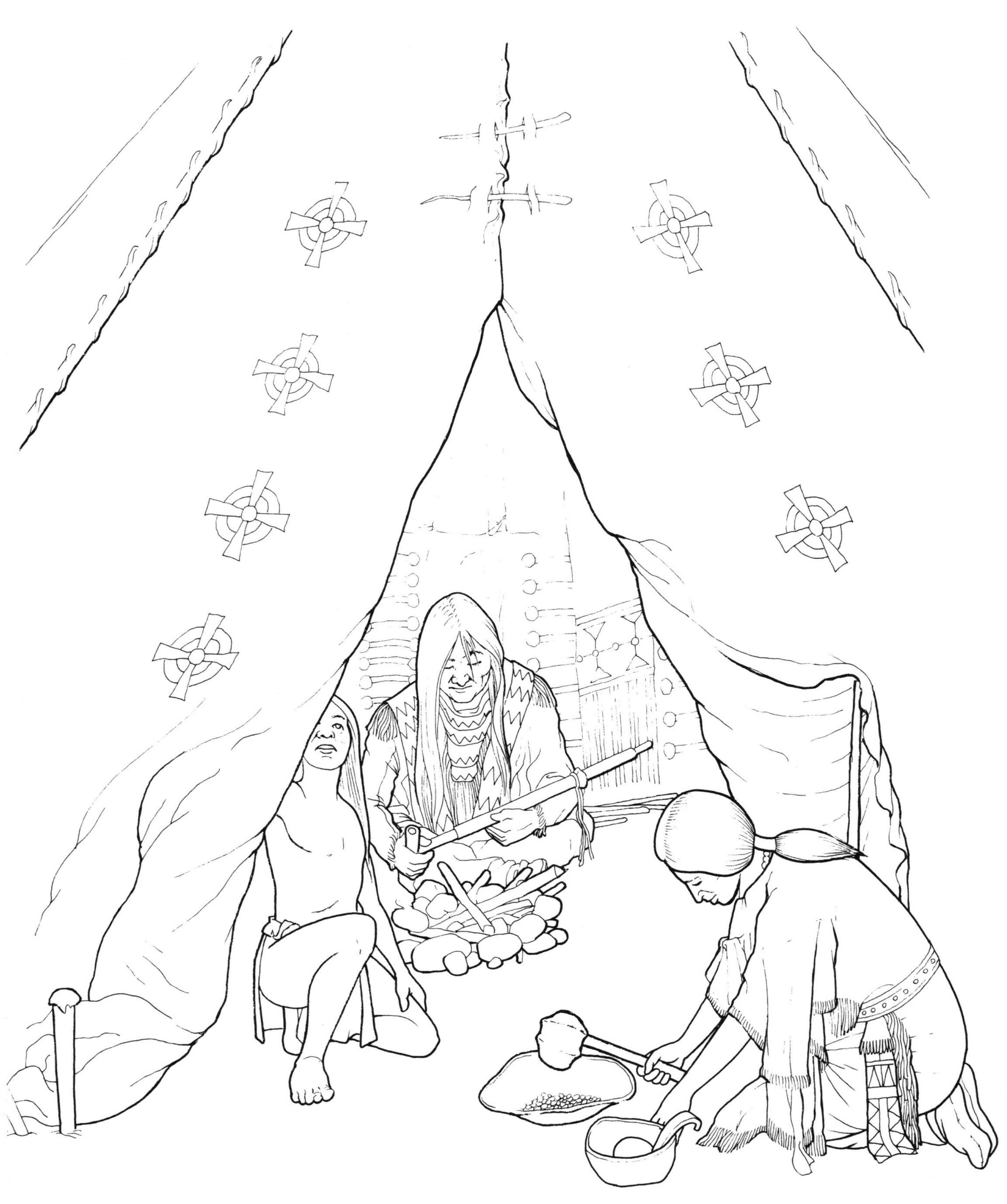

**Inside a Plains Indian Teepee** The woman in this scene is preparing pemmican, made of sun-dried buffalo meat, sliced thin, buffalo fat, marrow grease, and dried, pitted wild cherries. She is pulverizing all of these ingredients in a rawhide mortar with a stone pestle.

**Yosemite Indians Return to Camp** These Indians lived in the beautiful valley of present-day Yosemite National Park in California. They hunted in the mountains and fished in the swift streams. Their conical lodges were framed with cedar bark slabs.

**Northwest Indian Carves a Totem Pole** The tall cedar totem poles carved and painted by the Northwest Indians stood at the entrances to the homes of tribal members. The art of these Indians is renowned for its decorative qualities and its technical perfection.

**Hupa Indians of California** Acorns were an important food of the Hupas of northern California. They were collected and processed by the women, while the men did the hunting and fishing.

**Navaho Weavers and Silversmiths** The skill of Navaho silversmiths, who enjoy a worldwide reputation, has been developed since 1850. It was after the Spanish colonists introduced sheep into the southwestern United States that the Navaho became shepherds and skilled weavers of wool.

**Apache Costume, 18th Century** The man's fringed shirt, the woman's two-piece dress, and the high-topped moccasins are of native buckskin. The man's breachcloth and the glass beads were obtained from white traders.

**Hopi Snake Dance** A snake priest dances with a snake in his mouth, while another priest diverts the attention of the snake with a feather wand. A third priest gathers up a stray snake.

**Zuni Pueblo Potter** Many of the Pueblo woman's household utensils were of clay. She made her own large jars for carrying and storing water, her cooking pots, ladles, spoons, and serving bowls, and she was proud of their beauty and utility.

**Indians of the Southwest Desert** In the desert of the Southwest, where temperatures of more than 100 degrees are common, little clothing was needed by the native Indians. Women wore only a skirt and men wore a loin cloth. Painted faces and bodies were common.

**Folk Costumes of Guatemala** The Indians of each village wear a distinctive costume. Indian women weave many colorful garments on the stick-loom known to the people there since before Columbus arrived in the New World.

**The Aymara of the Andean Highlands** More than two miles above sea level, on the high plateau of Peru and Bolivia, the Aymara struggle to make a living in a harsh environment. They grow potatoes, net fish, and raise llamas to serve as burden carriers.

**The Warlike Jivaros** The Jivaro war leader of eastern Ecuador pictured here wears a headdress and cincture of bark cloth covered with toucan and blue chatterer's feathers and a necklace and amulets of puma teeth. The blowgun had a barrel of chonta palm smeared with resin, and a bone mouthpiece.

**Hunting on the South American Pampas** These Indians are hunting rhea—flightless, ostrichlike birds—with bolas. The bola consists of three rocks encased in rawhide at the ends of rawhide cords. It is thrown to entangle the legs of the target.

**Peruvian Indians at a Market** The weekly market day is the focal point of Andean Indian life, both economically and socially. Indian men go to market to trade livestock and visit with their friends. The women sell produce.

**Tehuelche Indians of South America** The Tehuelche lived and hunted the guanaco, an animal of the camel family, on the open grasslands of southern Argentina. Guanaco meat was their chief food, and guanaco hides were made into clothing and covers for their homes.

**The Cocopa Desert Dwellers** The homeland of the Cocopa people, one of the groups of Yuman Indians, was in northern Mexico, near the mouth of the Colorado River.

**The Huichol** A conservative mountain tribe of Mexico, the Huichol Indians lived in the mountain valleys of the state of Jalisco. They were farmers who grew beans, corn, and squash.

**Lucayan Indians of the Bahamas** This was the scene as the fleet of Christopher Columbus appeared off the Bahamas on October 18, 1492, to the amazement of the native Lucayan Indians. Later the Spaniards enslaved the Lucayans, who had vanished from the islands by the early seventeenth century.

**Indians of Tierra del Fuego** The Yahgan people, who lived in the southernmost region of South America, derived most of their food from seals, fish, and mussels. They wore very little clothing and lived in simple brush shelters.